Aroun the World

Travel Color by Number Coloring for Adults Numbered Places & Favorite Destinations For Relaxation and Stress Relief

Copyright © 2022

All rights reserved. No part of this publication may be reproduced, distributed, or transmitted in any form or by any means, including photocopying, recording, or other electronic or mechanical methods, without the prior written permission of the publisher

Our Color Palette Tips

1. **Colors corresponding to each number are shown on the back cover of the book. There are 25 colors total in this book, including one "Flesh Tone" color where you can choose any flesh tone!**
   Each number corresponds to a color shown on the back of the book. **There will sometimes be an asterisk (*) that corresponds to "Any Flesh Tone."**
   To the left of each image, there's a list of colors used within that particular image. Simply match the numbers on the images to the colors on the list. If you tear a page out of the book, you can simply use the color key on the back of the book to match your colors. If you don't have an exact color match, that's totally fine. Feel free to use a similar color or shade. Although this is a color by number book, it's completely okay to get creative and change up the colors listed. You can let your imagination run wild, and color the images with whichever colors you like and have. The numbers are here to be a guide and to allow you to color without having to focus your energy on choosing colors.

2. **If there are any spaces on an image without a number, you can go ahead and leave that space white (blank)**
   You can leave any space without a number white (blank), or you can fill that space in with any color you like. Another idea is to color that space in with a white color (for example, if you'd like to use a shiny white or a different shade of white on an image.)

3. **Bonus Images may have a slightly different color palette**
   Because the bonus images are from previous books with slightly different color palettes, they may include colors that aren't on the back of this book. Simply match them the best that you can, or choose completely different colors if you like. You are the artist and you are allowed to relax and enjoy!

Color By Number Tips

1. **Relax and have fun**
   Let your cares slip away as you color the images. Take your time. Coloring is a meditative activity and there's no wrong way to do it. Feel free to color as you listen to music, watch TV, lounge in bed- do whatever relaxes you most! You can also color while you're out and about- on the train or at a cafe- take the book with you anywhere you go. Coloring is therapeutic and is great for stress relief and relaxation!

2. **Choose your coloring tools**
   Everyone has their favorite coloring markers, crayons, pencils, pens- even paints! Feel free to color with any tool that you like! If you choose markers or paints, **we recommend putting a blank sheet of paper or cardboard behind each image, so that your colors don't run onto the next image.**

3. **Test out your colors**
   Feel free to test out your colors on our Color Test Sheets at the back, and use our Custom Color Chart to make the color choices your own!

Relax and Enjoy!

1. Black

4. Brown

5. Dark Brown

6. Tan

7. Peach

8. Red

15. Green

16. Dark Green

19. Blue

20. Dark Blue

∗. Any Flesh Tone

Arashiyama Bamboo Grove, Japan

4. Brown

5. Dark Brown

6. Tan

8. Red

10. Orange

12. Yellow

13. Golden Yellow

14. Light Yellow

15. Green

16. Dark Green

17. Aqua Green

18. Light Blue

19. Blue

22. Violet

24. Vivid Pink

Bagan, Myanmar

2. Gray

3. Dark Gray

4. Brown

5. Dark Brown

7. Peach

10. Orange

12. Yellow

13. Golden Yellow

15. Green

16. Dark Green

18. Light Blue

Bangkok, Thailand

2. Gray

3. Dark Gray

4. Brown

6. Tan

7. Peach

13. Golden Yellow

15. Green

16. Dark Green

18. Light Blue

19. Blue

23. Pink

Barcelona, Spain

2. Gray

3. Dark Gray

4. Brown

5. Dark Brown

6. Tan

12. Yellow

15. Green

16. Dark Green

18. Light Blue

Blue Lagoon, Iceland

4. Brown

5. Dark Brown

6. Tan

7. Peach

13. Golden Yellow

15. Green

16. Dark Green

17. Aqua Green

18. Light Blue

24. Vivid Pink

Bora Bora, French Polynesia

2. Gray

3. Dark Gray

4. Brown

5. Dark Brown

6. Tan

7. Peach

8. Red

10. Orange

12. Yellow

14. Light Green

15. Green

18. Light Blue

19. Blue

20. Dark Blue

21. Lilac

22. Violet

23. Pink

24. Vivid Pink

Cape Town, South Africa

2. Gray

3. Dark Gray

4. Brown

5. Dark Brown

6. Tan

7. Peach

8. Red

9. Orange Red

10. Orange

12. Yellow

13. Golden Yellow

14. Light Green

15. Green

17. Aqua Green

18. Light Blue

19. Blue

21. Lilac

22. Violet

23. Pink

24. Vivid Pink

Cappadocia, Turkey

2. Gray

3. Dark Gray

4. Brown

5. Dark Brown

6. Tan

7. Peach

8. Red

9. Orange Red

10. Orange

12. Yellow

13. Golden Yellow

14. Light Green

15. Green

17. Aqua Green

18. Light Blue

19. Blue

20. Dark Blue

21. Lilac

22. Violet

23. Pink

24. Vivid Pink

Marrakech, Morocco

4. Brown

5. Dark Brown

6. Tan

10. Orange

14. Light Green

15. Green

16. Dark Green

18. Light Blue

Mù Cang Chải, Vietnam

2. Gray

3. Dark Gray

4. Brown

5. Dark Brown

6. Tan

7. Peach

8. Red

10. Orange

12. Yellow

14. Light Green

15. Green

16. Dark Green

17. Aqua Green

18. Light Blue

19. Blue

21. Lilac

22. Violet

Venice, Italy

10. Orange

14. Light Green

17. Aqua Green

18. Light Blue

19. Blue

20. Dark Blue

Patagonia, Chile

2. Gray

3. Dark Gray

4. Brown

5. Dark Brown

6. Tan

7. Peach

8. Red

9. Orange Red

10. Orange

14. Light Green

15. Green

16. Dark Green

18. Light Blue

19. Blue

21. Lilac

22. Violet

Lake Bled, Slovenia

2. Gray

3. Dark Gray

4. Dark Brown

5. Dark Brown

6. Tan

10. Peach

12. Yellow

15. Green

16. Dark Green

17. Aqua Green

18. Light Blue

19. Blue

Galápagos Islands, Ecuador

2. Gray

3. Dark Gray

4. Brown

5. Dark Brown

6. Tan

14. Light Green

15. Green

16. Dark Green

17. Aqua Green

18. Light Blue

Kauai, Hawaii

6. Tan

7. Peach

12. Yellow

15. Green

16. Dark Green

17. Aqua Green

18. Light Blue

19. Blue

Santorini, Greece

2. Gray

3. Dark Gray

4. Brown

5. Dark Brown

6. Tan

8. Red

10. Orange

12. Yellow

13. Golden Yellow

15. Green

18. Light Blue

19. Blue

Forbidden City, Beijing, China

4. Brown

7. Peach

8. Red

10. Orange

12. Yellow

13. Golden Yellow

14. Light Green

15. Green

16. Dark Green

18. Light Blue

19. Blue

21. Lilac

22. Violet

23. Pink

Great Barrier Reef, Australia

4. Brown

5. Dark Brown

6. Tan

7. Peach

8. Red

12. Yellow

18. Light Blue

19. Blue

20. Dark Blue

*. Any Flesh Tone

Isla Holbox, Mexico

2. Gray

3. Dark Gray

6. Tan

12. Yellow

15. Green

16. Dark Green

18. Light Blue

19. Blue

21. Lilac

Isle of Skye, Scotland

2. Gray

3. Dark Gray

4. Brown

5. Dark Brown

6. Tan

7. Peach

8. Red

10. Orange

12. Yellow

14. Light Green

15. Green

16. Dark Green

18. Light Blue

19. Blue

21. Lilac

22. Violet

23. Pink

24. Vivid Pink

Lake Tekapo, New Zealand

1. Black

2. Gray

3. Dark Gray

4. Brown

5. Dark Brown

6. Tan

12. Yellow

15. Green

16. Dark Green

18. Light Blue

Serengeti National Park, Tanzania

2. Gray

3. Dark Gray

6. Tan

7. Peach

15. Green

16. Dark Green

18. Light Blue

23. Pink

Paris, France

4. Brown

6. Tan

7. Peach

18. Light Blue

Giza, Egypt

4. Brown

6. Tan

7. Peach

9. Orange Red

10. Orange

12. Yellow

13. Golden Yellow

18. Light Blue

Jaipur, India

2. Gray

3. Dark Gray

4. Brown

5. Dark Brown

6. Tan

7. Peach

9. Orange Red

10. Orange

12. Yellow

13. Golden Yellow

15. Green

17. Aqua Green

18. Light Blue

19. Blue

21. Lilac

23. Pink

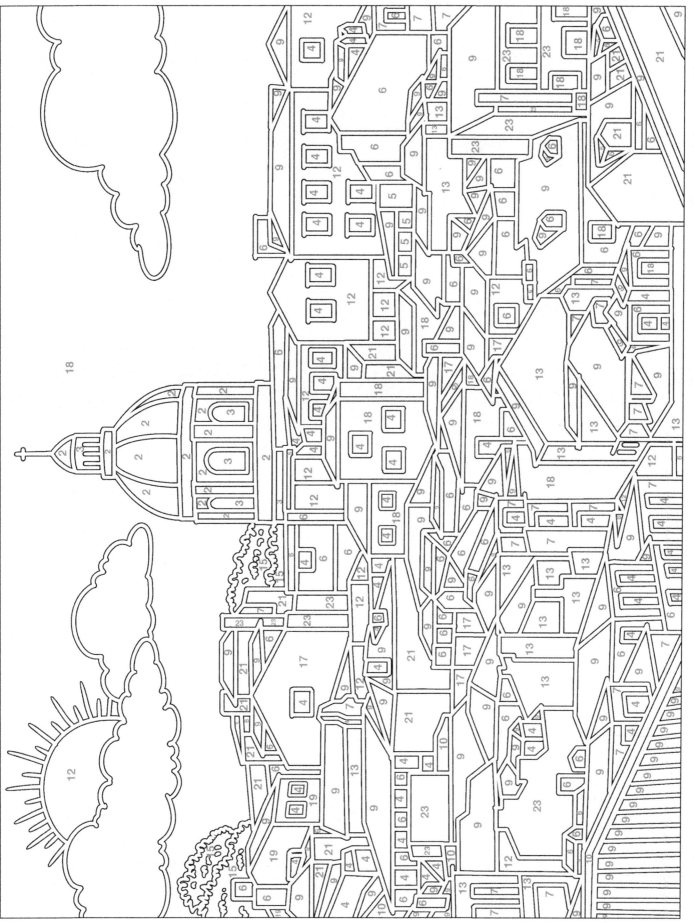

Lisbon, Portugal

2. Gray

3. Dark Gray

4. Brown

6. Tan

7. Peach

8. Red

14. Light Green

15. Green

17. Aqua Green

18. Light Blue

Lofoten Islands, Norway

2. Gray

3. Dark Gray

4. Brown

6. Tan

14. Light Green

15. Green

16. Dark Green

18. Light Blue

19. Blue

Machu Picchu, Peru

2. Gray

3. Dark Gray

4. Brown

6. Tan

7. Peach

8. Red

9. Orange Red

10. Orange

12. Yellow

13. Golden Yellow

15. Green

16. Dark Green

18. Light Blue

19. Blue

21. Lilac

22. Violet

23. Pink

Prague, Czech Republic

2. Gray

3. Dark Gray

6. Tan

9. Orange Red

10. Orange

17. Aqua Green

18. Light Blue

19. Blue

21. Lilac

22. Violet

23. Pink

24. Vivid Pink

Vancouver, Canada

ENJOY BONUS IMAGES FROM SOME OF OUR OTHER FUN COLOR BY NUMBER BOOKS!

FIND ALL OF OUR BOOKS ON AMAZON

National Parks
Volume 2
Color By Number
Coloring Book for Adults

2. Gray

3. Dark Gray

4. Brown

5. Dark Brown

8. Red

12. Yellow

15. Green

18. Light Blue

19. Blue

22. Violet

23. Pink

Wrangell- St Elias National Park - Alaska

Fantasy Landscapes
Mosaic Color By Number Coloring Book for Adults

1. Black
2. Golden
3. Light Red
4. Medium Red
5. Red
6. Dark Red
7. Lemon Yellow
8. Light Yellow
9. Yellow
10. Dark Yellow
11. Bright Orange
12. Light Orange
13. Medium Orange
14. Orange
15. Dark Orange
16. Chocolate
17. Light Brown
18. Medium Brown
19. Brown
20. Dark Brown
21. Neon Green
22. Light Green
23. Medium Green
24. Green
25. Army Green

26. Dark Green
27. Peach
28. Light Pink
29. Medium Pink
30. Pink
31. Hot Pink
32. Dark Pink
33. Medium Purple
34. Purple
35. Light Violet
36. Soft Violet
37. Violet
38. Dark Violet
39. Baby Blue
40. Sky Blue
41. Light Blue
42. Medium Blue
43. Blue
44. Dark Blue
45. Navy Blue
46. Beige
47. Light Gray
48. Medium Gray
49. Gray
50. Dark Gray

Flowers and Gardens
Color By Number
Coloring Book for Adults

4. Brown

6. Tan

7. Peach

9. Orange Red

12. Yellow

14. Light Green

15. Green

16. Dark Green

17. Aqua Green

18. Light Blue

21. Lilac

23. Pink

24. Vivid Pink

Beautiful Cities and Landmarks
Color by Number
Mosaic World Geography
Coloring Book For Adults

1. Gray

2. Medium Gray

3. Dark Gray

4. Dark Violet

5. Violet

6. Light Violet

7. Green

8. Dark Brown

9. Light Brown

10. Light Blue

11. Light Gray

12. Beige

13. Sky Blue

14. Light Pink

15. Navy Blue

16. Yellow

17. Orange

Beach Coloring Book
Large Print Summer Fun
Mosaic Color By Numbers

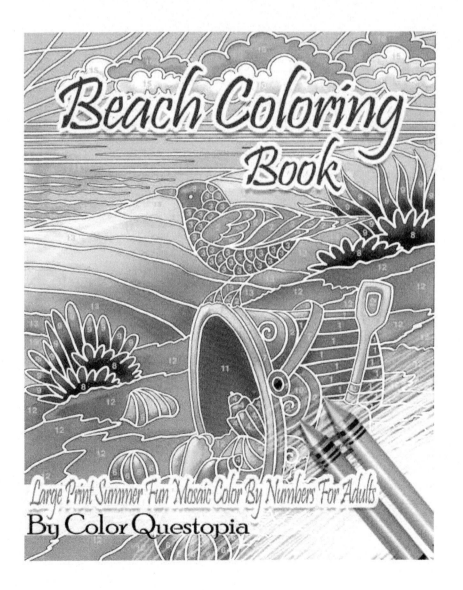

1. Light Violet

2. Violet

3. Medium Green

4. Light Green

5. Green

6. Dark Green

7. Beige

8. Brown

9. Army Green

10. Yellow

11. Pink

12. Light Gray

13. Baby Blue

14. Light Blue

15. Bright Orange

16. White

17. Sky Blue

Custom Color Chart

Medium: _ _ _ _ _ _ _ _   Brand: _ _ _ _ _ _ _ _

1. Black

2. Gray

3. Dark Gray

4. Brown

5. Dark Brown

6. Tan

7. Peach

8. Red

9. Orange Red

10. Orange

11. Light Yellow

12. Yellow

13. Golden Yellow

14. Light Green

15. Green

16. Dark Green

17. Aqua Green

18. Light Blue

19. Blue

20. Dark Blue

21. Lilac

22. Violet

23. Pink

24. Vivid Pink

* Flesh Tone

Custom Color Chart

Medium: _ _ _ _ _ _ _ _   Brand: _ _ _ _ _ _ _ _

1. _____

2. _____

3. _____

4. _____

5. _____

6. _____

7. _____

8. _____

9. _____

10. _____

11. _____

* 12. _____

13. _____

14. _____

15. _____

16. _____

17. _____

18. _____

19. _____

20. _____

21. _____

22. _____

23. _____

24. _____

* _____

Printed in Great Britain
by Amazon